W9-BTH-078

A New True Book

EXPERIMENTS WITH ANIMAL BEHAVIOR

By Ovid K. Wong, Ph. D.

CHILDRENS PRESS ®

CHICAGO

Juv QL 751.5. W66
1988t

Red squirrel collects pine cones.

*This book is dedicated to two persons who
are so far away and yet so close to me —
DAVID and LORRI*

PHOTO CREDITS

AP/Wide World Photos, Inc.—34

Journalism Services:
© J/J Clark—4 (bottom right)
© Harvey Moshman—44 (top left)
© Steve Sumner—10 (bottom)
© Scott Wanner—30 (right)

© Peter B. Louie—Cover, 13 (2 photos), 14
(2 photos), 17 (2 photos), 19 (2 photos),
22 (2 photos), 28 (3 photos), 32, 37 (2 photos),
43 (2 photos)

© Norma Morrison—4 (bottom left), 30 (left), 38
(left), 41, 44 (top right and bottom left)

Root Resources:
© Louise K. Broman—25 (bottom)
© MacDonald Photography—44 (bottom right)
© Mary Root—23

Tom Stack & Associates:
© Terry Ashley—7
© John Cancalosi—10 (top)
© T. J. Cawley—26 (bottom left)
© J. Gerlach—26 (top)
© Thomas Kitchin—2
© Brian Parker—4 (top), 9
© Rod Planck—26 (bottom left)
© John Shaw—25 (top)
© Tom Stack—38 (right)

Cover—Experiment with mealworms

Library of Congress Cataloging-in-Publication Data

Wong, Ovid K.
    Experiments with animal behavior / by Ovid K. Wong.
        p.   cm. — (A New true book)
    Includes index.
    Summary: Instructions for a variety of simple
experiments examining the reflex, instinctive, and
conditioned behavior of such animals as mealworms,
fruit flies, and goldfish.
    ISBN 0-516-01214-2
    1. Animal behavior—Experiments—Juvenile
literature. [1. Animal behavior—
Experiments. 2. Experiments.] I. Title.
QL751.5.W66   1988   87-33779
591.51—dc19   CIP
                                          AC

Childrens Press®, Chicago
Copyright ©1988 by Regensteiner Publishing Enterprises, Inc.
All rights reserved. Published simultaneously in Canada.
Printed in the United States of America.
1 2 3 4 5 6 7 8 9 10 R 97 96 95 94 93 92 91 90 89 88

TABLE OF CONTENTS

Scientists may study animal
behavior in order to better
understand human behavior.

INTRODUCTION

Many people are interested in human behavior. What makes a human think and act in a particular fashion? To better understand human behavior scientists often closely study animal behaviors.

Scientists have concluded that stimulus and response are two important elements in behavior patterns. A stimulus is a change in the environment that affects the organism. A response is an activity of the organism produced by the stimulus. For example, a water flea bumps into a stone and backs up.

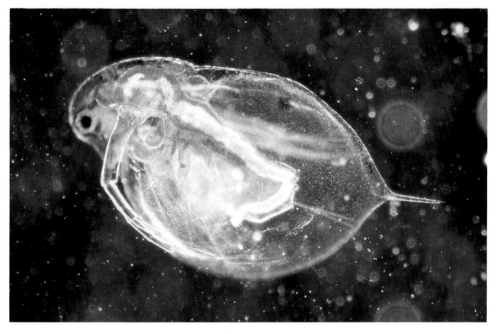

Water flea or daphnia

Let us examine what has happened here. To the water flea, the stone is an obstacle. Therefore, it is a stimulus in the flea's environment. The water flea's response is to back up and avoid the stone.

From this example, we see that stimulus (the stone) produces response (backing up).

Animal behavior involves activity changes over time. Some of these changes occur either so quickly or so slowly that we fail to recognize them. For that reason careful observation and recording are the keys to doing effective experiments in animal behavior.

Closing your eyes when you hit the water is a simple reflex.

SIMPLE REFLEX BEHAVIOR

Simple reflexes are automatic responses that require no thought. For example, your eyelid automatically closes just before a dust particle gets

Here are two examples of simple reflex behavior. When the nonpoisonous hognose snake is touched or threatened, it will immediately roll over and pretend to be dead. In a snowball fight, people will turn away from an oncoming snowball and use their hands to protect themselves.

into your eye. That is an example of a simple reflex behavior. All animals respond to light, temperature, humidity, and physical touch.

One way to observe the way an animal shows simple reflex behavior is to watch the way mealworms (the larva of a type of beetle) respond to light.

EXPERIMENT WITH MEALWORMS

Equipment:
  dishcloth
  aluminum pie pan
  string
  mealworms (buy at a pet
  store or a bait shop)

Stretch the dishcloth tightly over the pie pan and secure it with a string. Place about ten mealworms on the cloth. Put the pie pan in a well-lighted room. Observe what happens.

The mealworms should move through the cloth into the pan below. This behavior can be explained by the fact that mealworms do not like light. They therefore automatically try to escape the light.

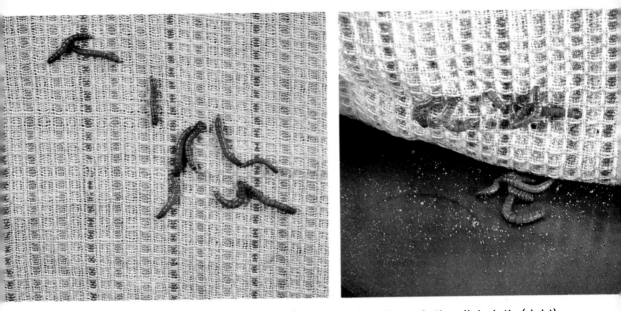

Mealworms on the dishcloth (left) and moving through the dishcloth (right)

In this experiment, the light was the stimulus, or change in the environment. The mealworms responded by moving away from the light.

You can verify this experiment by doing it again, this time leaving the lights off. Can you design another experiment to compare results?

Not all animals respond to light in the same way. Let's see how fruit flies respond to light.

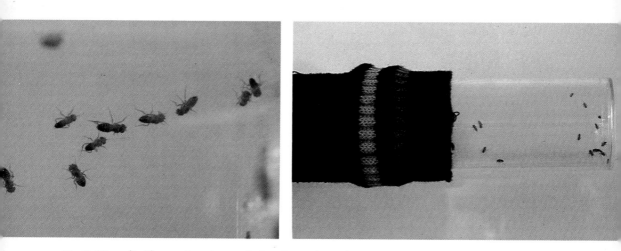

Fruit flies (left) moving toward the light (right)

EXPERIMENT WITH FRUIT FLIES

Equipment:
    fruit fly culture in a tube
    (available from a biological house)
    1 clean culture tube
    1 sock

Remove the plug from the culture tube and immediately place the empty culture tube over the first one. Use the sock to cover the culture tube that contains the flies. Observe what happens.

In a short time, the flies should have moved toward the light. In this experiment, the light was the stimulus and the fruit flies responded by moving toward the light.

If you wanted to attract a fruit fly, would you use the same technique that you would use if you wanted to attract a mealworm? Explain your answer.

Another experiment to test simple reflexes is to observe how fruit flies respond to cold temperature.

EXPERIMENT WITH TEMPERATURE

Equipment:
  fruit fly culture
  freezer

Place the fruit fly culture on its side in the freezer. After five to seven minutes, remove the culture and observe what happens.

At first, the flies were immobilized by the sudden drop in temperature. In a short time, however, the flies became active again. This happened because the flies are cold-sensitive and become inactive at low temperatures. In this experiment, the sudden drop in temperature was the stimulus in the environment. The flies respond by becoming inactive.

You can also try this experiment by adjusting the amount of time you leave the fruit fly culture in the freezer. What happens if you freeze the culture for three minutes? For ten minutes? How long does it take for the flies to become active again? Can you explain the results?

You can observe reflex behavior by finding out how mealworms respond to humidity.

EXPERIMENT WITH HUMIDITY

Equipment:
round filter paper   petri dish
scissors   mealworms

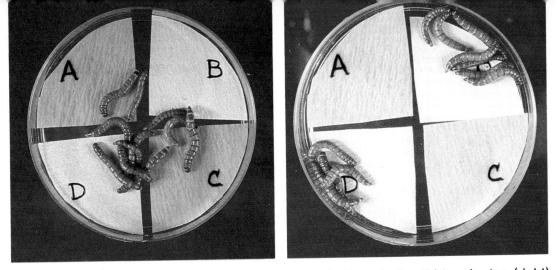

Mealworms before (left) and after thirty minutes (right)

Fold the filter paper in half twice. Open the paper and cut along the folded lines to obtain four equal sections. Mark the sections A, B, C, and D. Moisten sections A and C slightly and place them in the petri dish. Place the paper sections in the petri dish (the filter paper should be slightly smaller than the dish). Leave a narrow space between the sections.

Put ten mealworms in the center of the dish. Record what happens every minute for thirty minutes. Write down the number of mealworms on each paper section after thirty minutes.

At the end of thirty minutes, most of the mealworms should be on the dry sections B and D. Mealworms prefer dry areas over

17

wet areas. In this experiment, the moist sections of the paper were the stimulus. The mealworms that were put on the moist areas automatically responded by moving to a drier area.

Another experiment with animal reflex behavior demonstrates how sow bugs respond to temperature changes.

EXPERIMENT WITH SOW BUGS

Equipment:
  aluminum foil
  3 small thermometers
  2 bowls
  warm water
  ice cubes

  sow bugs (available from a biological supply house or by digging under a stone in the yard or in a forest preserve)

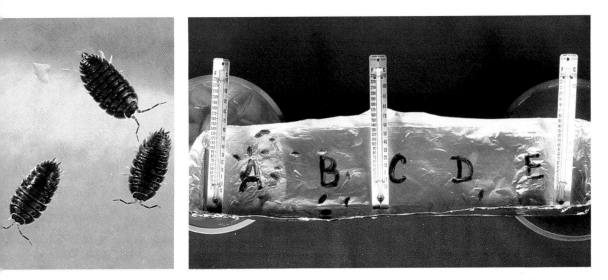
Sow bugs (left) and after the experiment has lasted fifteen minutes (right)

Fold aluminum foil to make a rectangular tray. Divide the tray into five equal parts. Label them A, B, C, D, and E. Fill one bowl with warm water and the other bowl with ice cubes. Make sure that one end of the tray touches the warm water. The other end touches the ice cubes. Put a thermometer at sections A, C, and E of the tray.

Place ten sow bugs in the C section. Observe and record the movement of the sow bugs every minute. Do this for thirty minutes.

More sow bugs probably moved toward the cold end of the tray. The bugs moved because sow bugs prefer cold climates.

19

For our final experiment in reflex behavior, we will observe how pill bugs respond to touch.

EXPERIMENT WITH PILL BUGS

Equipment:
pill bugs (available from
a biological supply house
or can be found under
stones or logs in the
backyard or in a forest
preserve)

Place five big pill bugs in a dish. Touch and poke the pill bugs with your finger. Observe what happens.

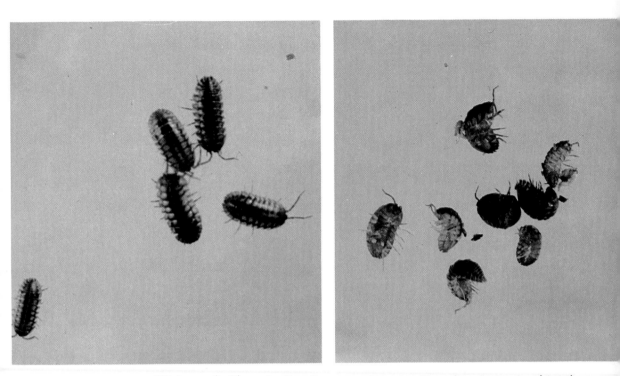

Pill bugs (left) and after the experiment with reflex behavior (right)

Each of the pill bugs should have rolled into a ball and then unrolled after a short time. The pill bugs respond to the stimulus (touch) by rolling into a ball.

Why do you think the pill bug rolled into a ball? Could it be to help escape an enemy? Do people usually respond to danger in the same way as a pill bug? Explain your answer.

INSTINCTIVE BEHAVIOR

Have you ever seen a squirrel burying a nut? The act of burying a nut is more complicated than the simple reflex of eye blinking. The squirrel must keep the nut in its mouth, find a hiding place, drop the nut in, and then cover it. How did the squirrel learn to do that? Did the parent teach it or did it learn from the other squirrels?

Squirrels demonstrate instinctive behavior when they bury nuts.

Studies have shown that a squirrel can hide nuts even if it has never seen another squirrel do this. This is a result of an inborn behavior that does not require previous learning. Behavior such as this is usually related to survival. Scientists call this an instinctive behavior.

An instinctive behavior is a chain of actions. Usually one instinctive action sets off another. The second action sets off a third action, and so forth. Instinctive behavior is usually characteristic of a particular species. For example, most spiders spin webs, but each species of spider spins its own kind

Most spiders spin webs, but each species spins its own kind of web.

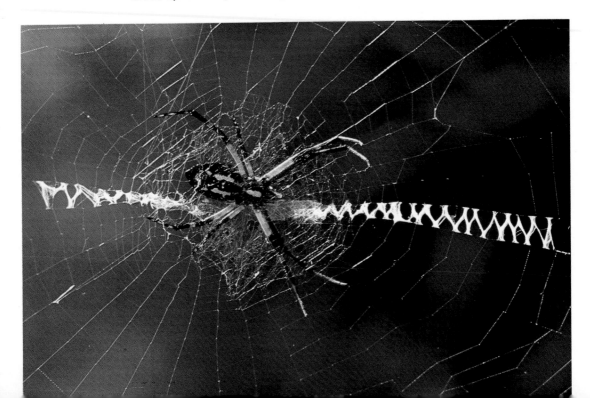

The cedar waxwing (above), the blue-winged warbler (below left), and the robin (below right) all build different kinds of nests for their young.

of web. In the same way most birds build nests, but each species of bird instinctively builds its own kind of nest.

Here is an experiment showing the instinctive behavior of butterfly larvae.

EXPERIMENT WITH BUTTERFLY LARVAE

Equipment:
   culture jar of butterfly
   larvae (available from a biological
   supply house)

Let the culture jar sit in an airy place. The larvae, or caterpillars, will grow by eating the food in the jar. After a little while the larvae will stop eating and will climb to the lid of the jar. Observe what happens.

The butterfly caterpillar or larvae (above left) demonstrates instinctive behavior when it spins its cocoon (left). The offspring of this butterfly will instinctively do the same things its parent did.

Each larva should have hung from the lid of the jar by silk threads. The larva will produce silk threads and wrap itself in a cocoon. After a few days you will see a butterfly breaking through the cocoon.

We know that the larva is behaving instinctively because it could not have learned this process from its parents. The larva is instinctively changing in order to survive.

HABIT-FORMING
BEHAVIOR

Do you know how to tie
shoelaces? Tying shoelaces
is a complicated action
that has to be learned.
Once you have learned how
to tie shoelaces, you can
do it automatically. When
a learned behavior becomes
automatic, it is called a

Tying your shoelaces and brushing your teeth
are learned activities that become habits.

habit. Many things that we
do every day are habits.
We brush our teeth, get
dressed, and walk to
school without thinking
much about all the actions
involved.

Here is an experiment to help show how a habit is formed. For this experiment you will need paper and pencil.

EXPERIMENT WITH HABIT-FORMING BEHAVIOR

Write your name as quickly as possible with the hand you do not normally use. If you are right-handed, use your left hand, and vice versa. Write your name in this way ten times each day for four weeks. Record what happens.

At the end of the fourth week your writing should have improved. You have formed the habit of writing with your other hand. However, if you do not practice, the habit can be forgotten.

With practice a right-handed person can learn to write with his left hand.

Can you explain how a habit is different from a reflex? Here is a clue. You can unlearn a habit. Can you unlearn a reflex?

CONDITIONED BEHAVIOR

In 1897 a Russian scientist, Ivan Pavlov, experimented to see if simple reflex responses could be changed. He experimented with dogs and their salivary reflexes. When a dog smells food, its salivary glands secrete saliva, making its mouth water. The flow of saliva is a response to the stimulus of the smell of food.

An experiment using goldfish will help illustrate conditioned behavior.

EXPERIMENT WITH GOLDFISH

Equipment:
  aquarium
  goldfish
  fish food
  a coin

Set up the aquarium. Feed the goldfish at the same time every day. Tap the side of the tank with a coin everytime you feed the fish. Do this for four weeks. At the end of the fourth week, tap the aquarium but bring no food. Observe what happens.

Goldfish at the beginning of the
experiment (left) and after four weeks
of training (above)

The fish should come to
the surface of the water
even though no food was
put into the tank. You had
developed a conditioned
behavior in the fish.

37

Humans can learn to play the piano or to do gymnastics.

LEARNING BEHAVIOR

Learning occurs when a person or animal develops new behaviors as a result of past experience. This experiment will show you how experience leads to learning.

A	B	C
Biz	Yes	John
Waab	Dog	And
Omt	Harry	Mary
Borl	House	Went
Das	Moon	To
Krunk	Two	The
Kul	Cold	Party
Hicw	Not	Together
Urg	Bet	Last
Vzt	Was	Night

EXPERIMENT WITH LEARNING

Cover columns B and C with a piece of paper. Read column A four times. Now without looking at column A, write on a separate piece of paper as many words as you can remember in the correct order. This time try the same thing with column B after covering columns A and C. Now cover columns A and B and try to remember column C. Which column is easiest to learn?

Column C was the easiest because it is in a word order that makes sense. Column A is the most difficult because it is just a list of letters not words. The fact that you have had experience with sentences helps you learn the column C words faster than the words in column A or B.

CONCLUSION

Experiments with animal
behavior can be interesting
when we see similarities
in human behavior. While
you continue to investigate
different animal behaviors,
don't forget to observe
your friends and even

With practice
athletes can
learn to jump
greater distances.

yourself. Notice the different ways that males and females carry their books. Study the seating choices of students in a library. Observe whether people tend to sit near the walls or in the middle of the room in a cafeteria.

The way people carry their books (left) and the seats they take in church (below) are examples of human behavior.

Look around you. Watch what people do. Are their responses the result of reflex, instinctive, conditioned, or learned behavior?

Assuming that people are free to behave in many different ways, why do you suppose they often behave in similar ways? These and other questions of behavior are waiting for someone to provide answers for them. You could just be the person to do that.

SOURCES OF MATERIALS

Most of the materials used in this book may be purchased from your local hardware store or supermarket. Live materials may be purchased from pet stores and bait shops. However, materials may also be ordered from the following sources:

Carolina Biological Supply Company
Burlington, North Carolina 27215
(800) 632-1231

Fisher Scientific Company
4901 W. LeMoyne Street
Chicago, Illinois 60651
(800) 621-4769

NASCO West Inc.
P.O. Box 3837
Modesto, California 95352
(209) 529-6957

WORDS YOU SHOULD KNOW

automatically(aw • tih • MAT • ik • lee) — acted from force of habit or without thinking

behavior(be • HAY • vyer) — one's manner of acting; conduct

cocoon(kuh • KOON) — the fine covering spun by insect larvae, as moths and silkworms, for protection until they mature

environment(en • VYE • ron • mint) — all conditions and influences surrounding an individual or organism that affects its growth and development

experience(ex • PEER • ee • ince) — knowledge of skill gained through one's own actions, observations, practice

fruit fly(FROOT FLYE) — one of various small flies (genus Drosophila) having larvae that feed on ripe and decayed fruit and vegetables

immobilized(im • MOH • bih • lyzed) — made unable to move

inborn(IN • born) — natural; inherited; existing since birth

instinctive(in • STINK • tiv) — to sense or act with natural abilities, not through learning or reasoning

larva (plural, larvae)(LAR • va) — the first stage in insect life after leaving the egg, developing into different form in its adult stage, as grubs into beetles or bees, maggots into flies

mealworm(MEEL • werm) — the larva of several beetles (genus Tenebrio) that infest and feed on flour products

observation(ob • zer • VAY • shun) — the act of noticing or watching

organism(OR • ga • nizm) — any living being, animal or plant; a form of life with all parts depending upon each other, and each having a certain function

Petri dish(PEE • tree DISH) — a round shallow glass or plastic dish with a loose cover at top and sides, used to hold bacteria cultures in laboratory research

pill bugs(PIL BUGZ) — any of various small insects (genus Armadillium) having shell-like coverings and seven pairs of legs

reflex(REE • flex) —an automatic movement, as eye blinking or sneezing

response(rih • SPONSS) —a reaction by an organism to a stiumulus or irritation

saliva(suh • LYVE • uh) —the fluid produced by the salivary glands in the mouth to moisten chewed food, aiding in swallowing and digesting

salivary glands(SAL • ih • vair • ee GLANDZ) —any of three pairs of glands in the mouth that release saliva

sow bugs(SAOW BUGZ) —any of several shell-covered oval- or round-shaped insects (genus Oniscus); also called "wood louse"

stimulus(STIM • yoo • lus) —anything that causes a response

survival(ser • VIVE • il) —the act of remaining alive

technique(tek • NEEK) —a skill or method used in performing a task, developed through practice and ability

INDEX

About the author

Ovid K. Wong *earned his B.Sc. degree in biology from the University of Alberta, Edmonton, Canada, his M.Ed. in curriculum from the University of Washington, Seattle, and his Ph.D. in science education from the University of Illinois, Urbana-Champaign. He is currently the curriculum specialist for science, health, and outdoor education with school district #65 in Evanston, Illinois. Since 1984 he has served as a consultant for the Illinois State Board of Education and the State Board of Higher Education. He also taught science at the Center for Talent Development, Northwestern University. In 1987 he was appointed to serve on the Board of Directors, Chicago Heart Association, and to chair the Science Advisory Committee, Educational Services Center of North Cook County.*

Dr. Wong's work has appeared on public television and in such journals as Science Teacher, American Biology Teacher, ISTA Spectrum, The Bilingual Journal, *and a number of professional newsletters. Dr. Wong is the author of* A Glossary of Biology, Your Body and How It Works, Giant Pandas, Prehistoric People, *and* Experiments in Animal Behavior.